TOPIC BOX

Transport

Paul Bennett

Wayland

Titles in this Series

This book was prepared for Wayland (Publishers) Ltd
by Globe Education, Nantwich, Cheshire

Design concept by Pinpoint
Book design by Steven Wheele Design
Artwork by Nick Hawken

First published in 1996 by
Wayland (Publishers) Ltd
61 Western Road, Hove
East Sussex BN3 1JD

Printed and bound in Italy by
L.E.G.O. S.p.A., Vincenza

British Library Cataloguing in Publication Data

Bennett, Paul
Transport. – (Topic Box Series)
I. Title II. Series
388

ISBN 0 7502 1606 9

Picture acknowledgements
Eye Ubiquitous 11 (A Carrell), 12 (Christopher Portway), 14 (Julia Wateron)
Genesis 28, 29
Quadrant 25t, 25b, 27
Robert Harding 15 (Vanderharst), 16-17
Tony Stone 7 (David Woodfall), 8 (Dan Morley), 9 (Simon McComb), 26 (Dan Ham)
Wayland Picture Library 4 (and back cover), 4-5, 5, 7 (Jimmy Holmes), 10, 13, 17 (and title page), 18, 19, 20-21, 21, 24
Zefa 23 (B Abraham)

Contents

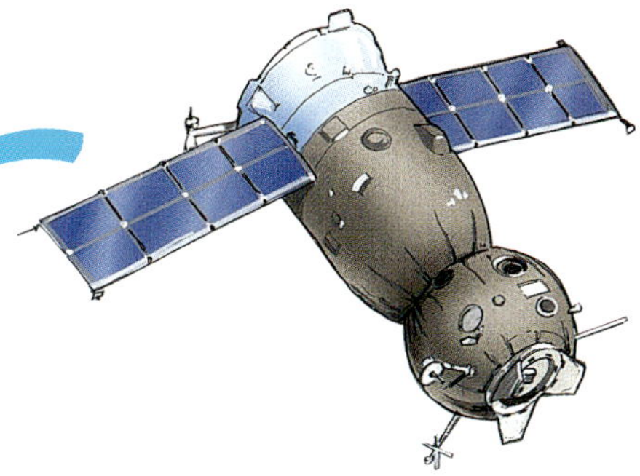

Kinds of Transport

Transport is very important for daily life. It allows you to travel to school, bring home the shopping, or to go on holiday.

Without transport, factories would not receive materials to make into goods, and the goods could not be transported to the shops for us to buy them.

There are three main types of transport allowing travel over land, over water and through the air.

(Below) Some methods of transport are slower than others.

(Left) Aircraft move people and goods to remote places.

Transport time line.

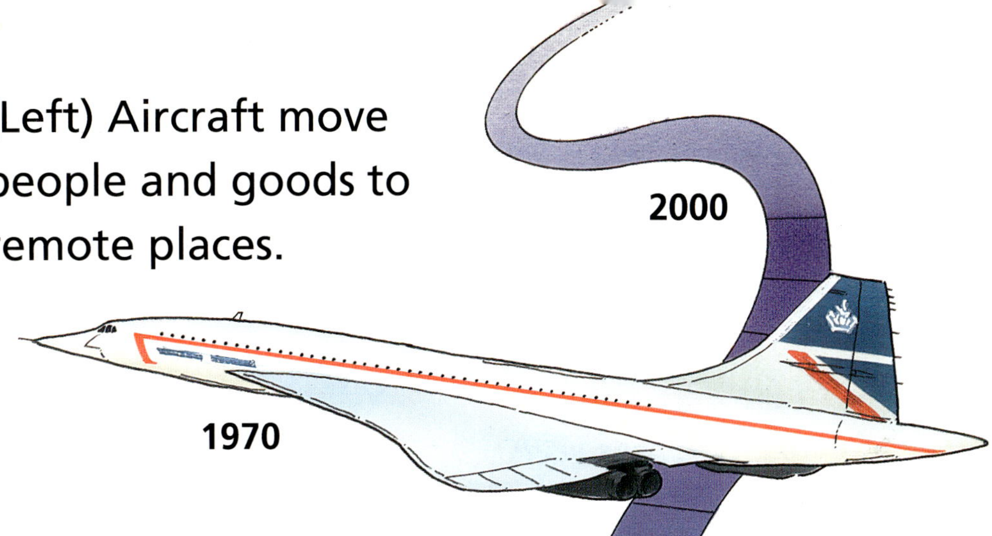

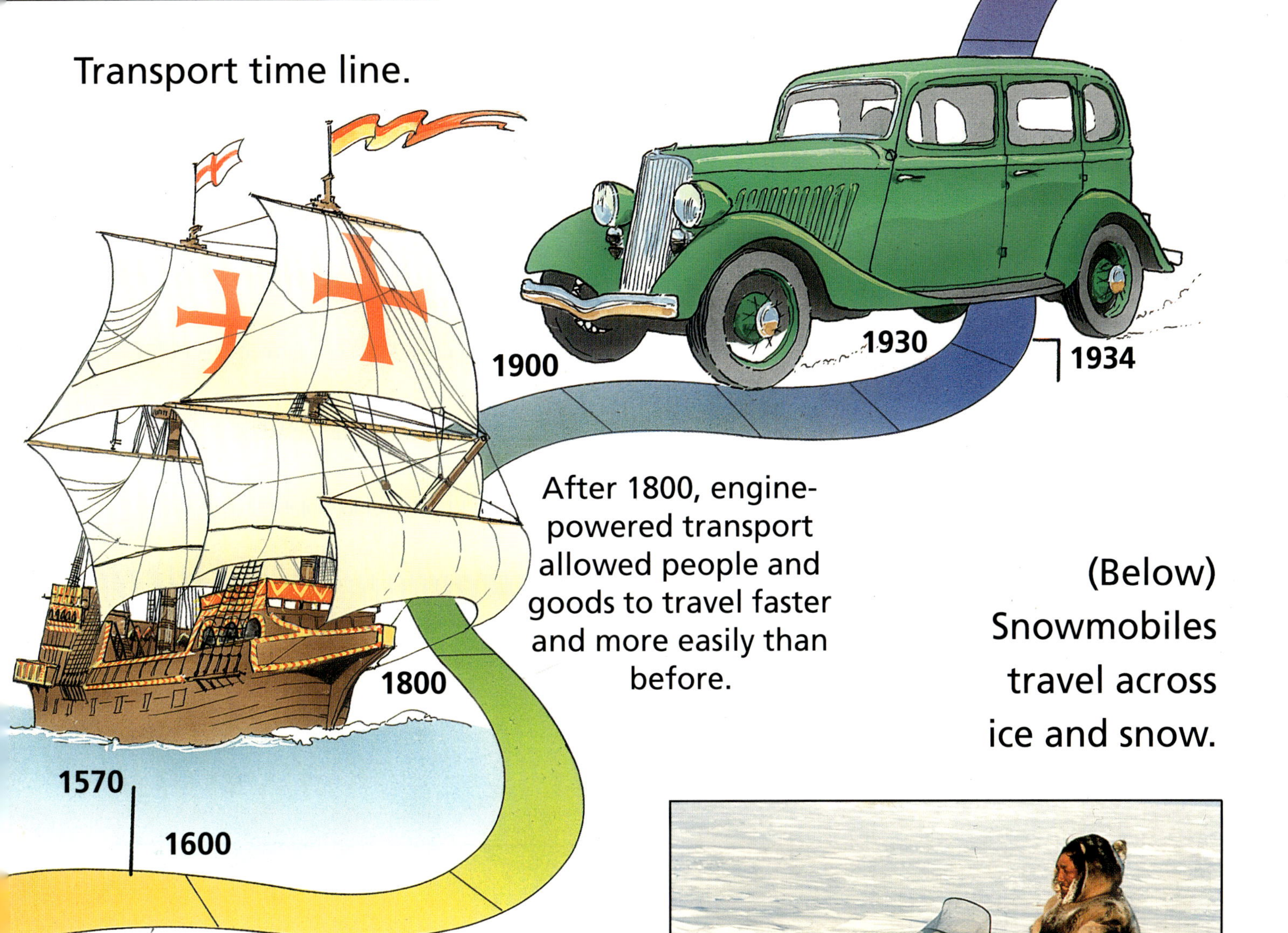

After 1800, engine-powered transport allowed people and goods to travel faster and more easily than before.

(Below) Snowmobiles travel across ice and snow.

Before the nineteenth century, transport relied on wind, water currents or the muscle power of people or animals.

On the Road

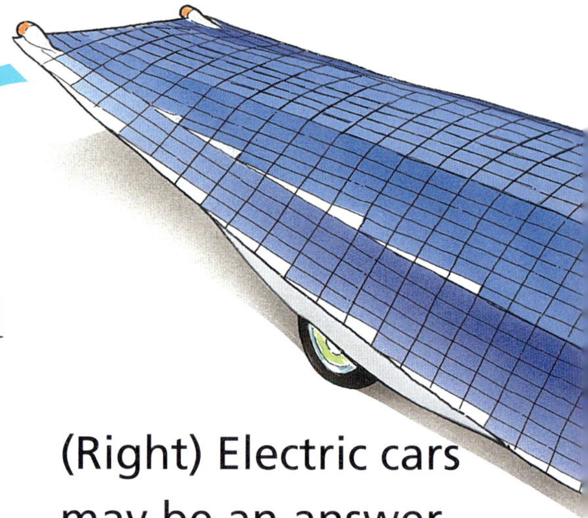

Wheeled vehicles are by far the commonest kind of transport. Cars, buses and lorries transport goods and passengers at high speed. A network of roads connects country, town and city, so people can travel easily to where they want to go. They can also travel whenever they choose.

(Right) Electric cars may be an answer to the pollution problem. This car makes electricity from sunlight.

But the centres of towns and cities are often full of slow-moving traffic, and the air is polluted with poisonous fumes from the engines.

(Right) In Australia, long 'road trains' transport goods to out-of-the-way places.

(Right) City centres are often blocked with traffic like this one in Japan.

(Below) The fumes from car engines are poisonous, particularly for young children in push-chairs.

On Two Wheels

The bicycle is a popular form of transport. It can be used for fun as well as for travelling to school or work. Bicycles do not pollute the air and they help to keep you fit and healthy.

hobby-horse, about 1800

Motor bikes or motor cycles have engines that allow people to travel fast. Like bicycles, they are a good way of travelling through busy city streets.

velocipede, 1830s

In China, millions of people travel to work on bicycles or motor cycles.

(Left) These motor cycles are built for speed. On the track they reach speeds of up to 250 kilometres per hour.

penny-farthing,
1870s

(Right) A mountain bike has strong wheels so that it can travel over bumpy ground. The gears make cycling up and down hills easier.

safety cycle,
1880s

Moulton bike,
1960s

The history of the bicycle from hobby-horse to racing bike.

racing bike,
1970s

On the Rails

Trains can carry heavier loads than lorries and many more passengers than buses. They run on tracks and so cannot deliver to your door.

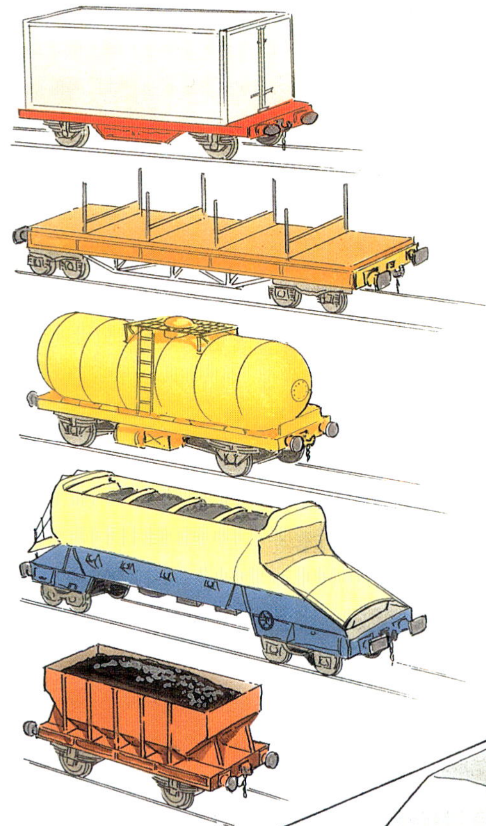

High-speed trains transport people between cities where underground railways are often the quickest method of getting around.

In some city streets, electric trams provide quiet transport with no exhaust fumes.

(Left) San Francisco in California, USA, is famous for its cable cars.

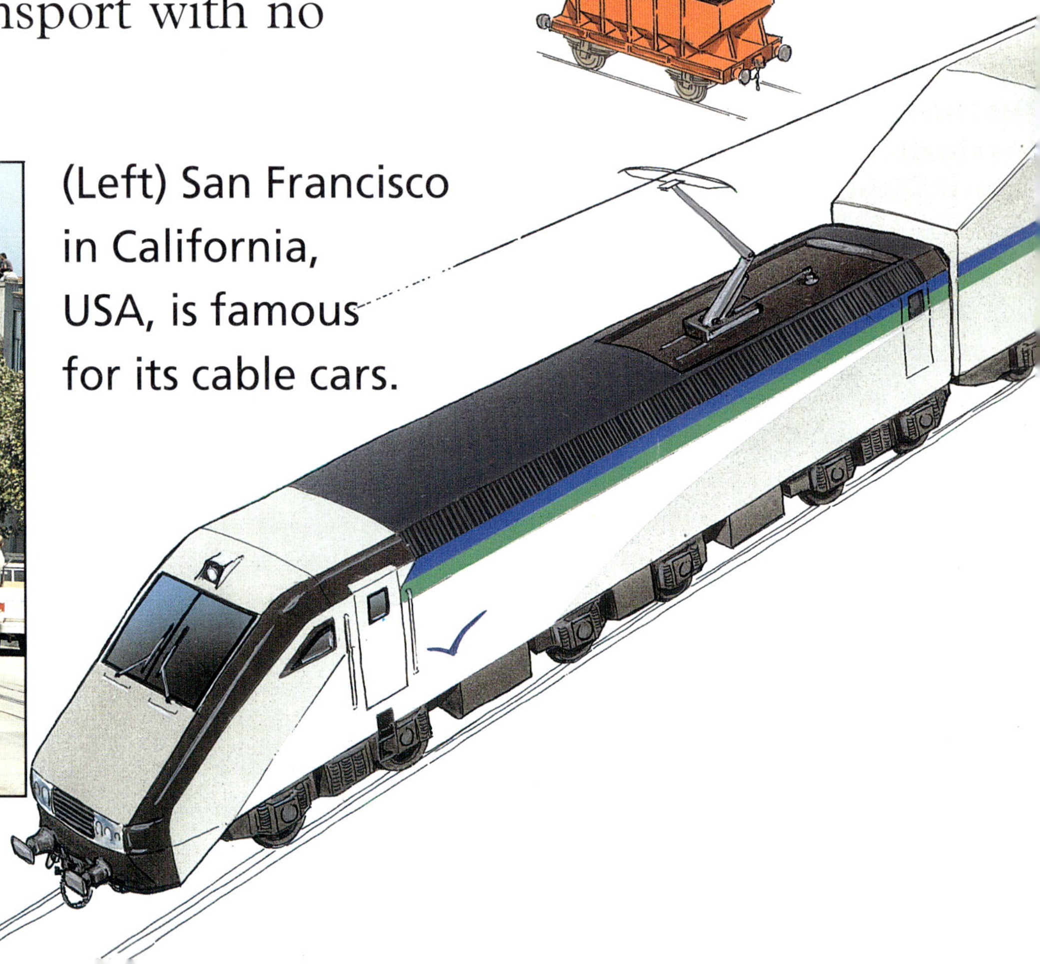

(Right) Sydney in Australia has a monorail system that travels above the busy city streets.

(Left) Some of the special railway cars used for carrying freight.

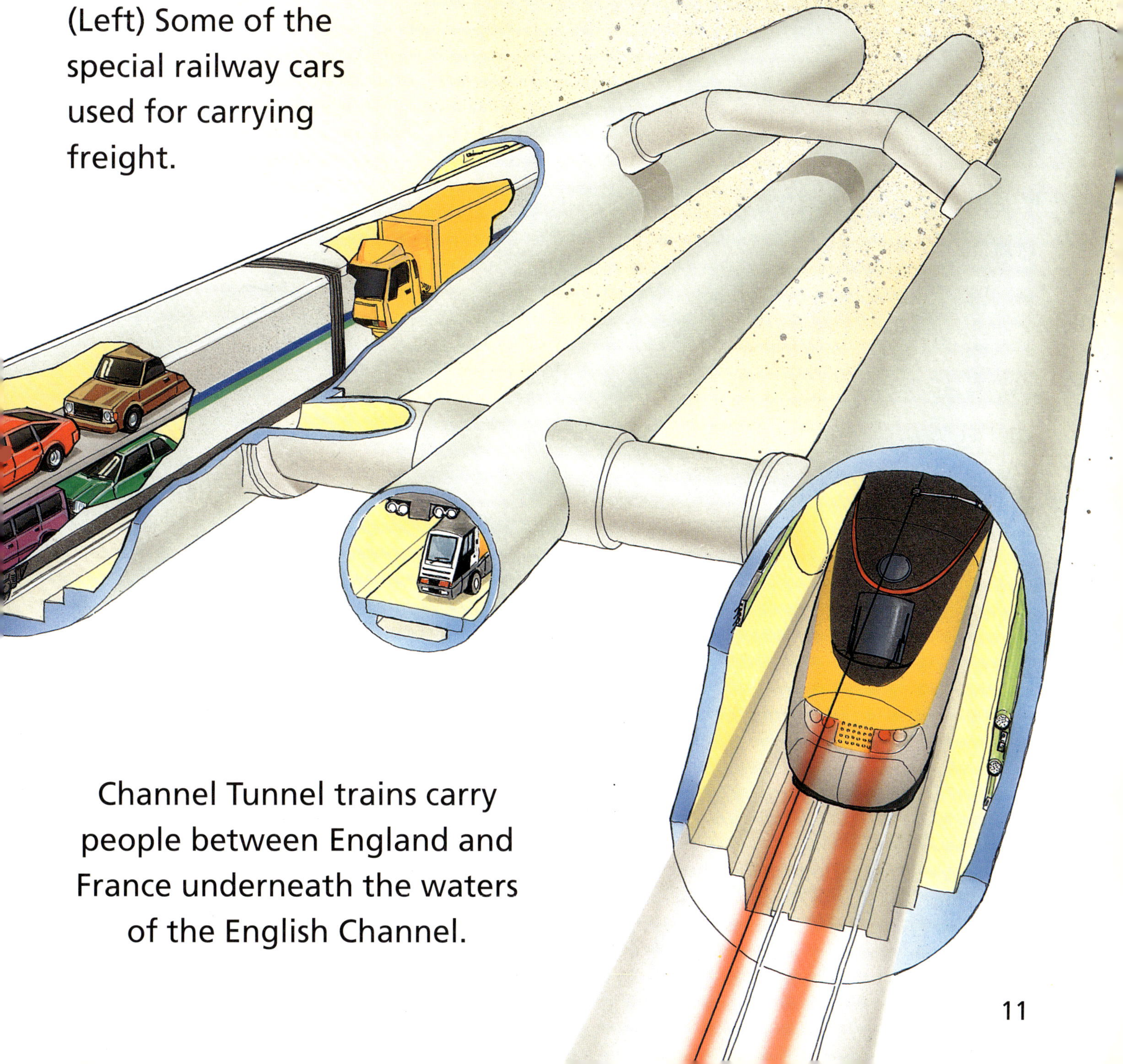

Channel Tunnel trains carry people between England and France underneath the waters of the English Channel.

Animal Power

Animals have long been used for transport. When they carry loads, they are called pack animals or beasts of burden. Horses, donkeys, elephants, camels, llamas and oxen are all used in this way.

Pack animals are used in places that do not have roads, such as mountains, jungles and deserts.

Animals are also harnessed to carts, carriages and sledges.

An age-old method of moving goods is to carry them yourself!

(Right) Huskies are still used to haul sledges over the Arctic ice.

(Right) In many countries, animal-drawn carts are an important means of transport.

Camels are used as pack animals in desert areas.

Going Up!

Some ways of travelling have no need of roads or rails.

Lifts and escalators allow people to move from floor to floor inside a tall building. In a skyscraper, a lift will carry you from the ground floor to the very top of the building.

In mountain regions, cable cars and chairlifts fastened to strong wires, take people where it is too steep or difficult to build roads or railways.

(Left) Escalators are a kind of moving staircase. They move people from one level to another.

(Above) A chairlift takes the effort out of climbing a mountain.

(Left) After the first lift was invented in 1854, people started to build skyscrapers with many floors.

Fun on the Water

Many people enjoy a day out having fun on the water. Different types of boats are used on rivers, canals, lakes and around the coast. Some have sails and are driven by the wind, others have oars, paddles or poles to move them around.

Motorboats speed across the water driven by powerful engines. Sometimes they tow water-skiers. Jet skis are like small motorboats with a kind of handlebar for steering.

canoe

catamaran

Having fun on the water using different kinds of power.

(Left) Sailing clubs organize races for their members.

jet ski

paraglider

pedalo

(Left) Safety comes first where boats are concerned. Each member of this family is wearing a life-jacket. They also check the distress flares before setting sail.

Ocean Travel

Journeys across oceans can take weeks or even months. Ocean going ships must be specially built for ocean travel.

Ocean liners are passenger ships that carry tourists on holiday cruises all over the world.

Cargo ships transport goods from one country to another. They are large, slow and carry huge cargoes. Some ships carry cargo in metal boxes called containers. These can be lifted straight off the ship on to lorries.

(Right) Ocean liners are like floating hotels. Passengers on board enjoy many luxuries.

(Above) Hovercraft travel on a cushion of air. They carry vehicles and passengers on short ocean crossings.

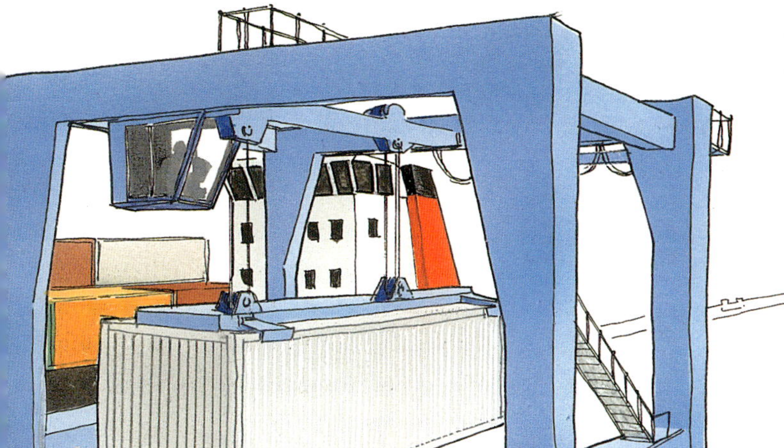
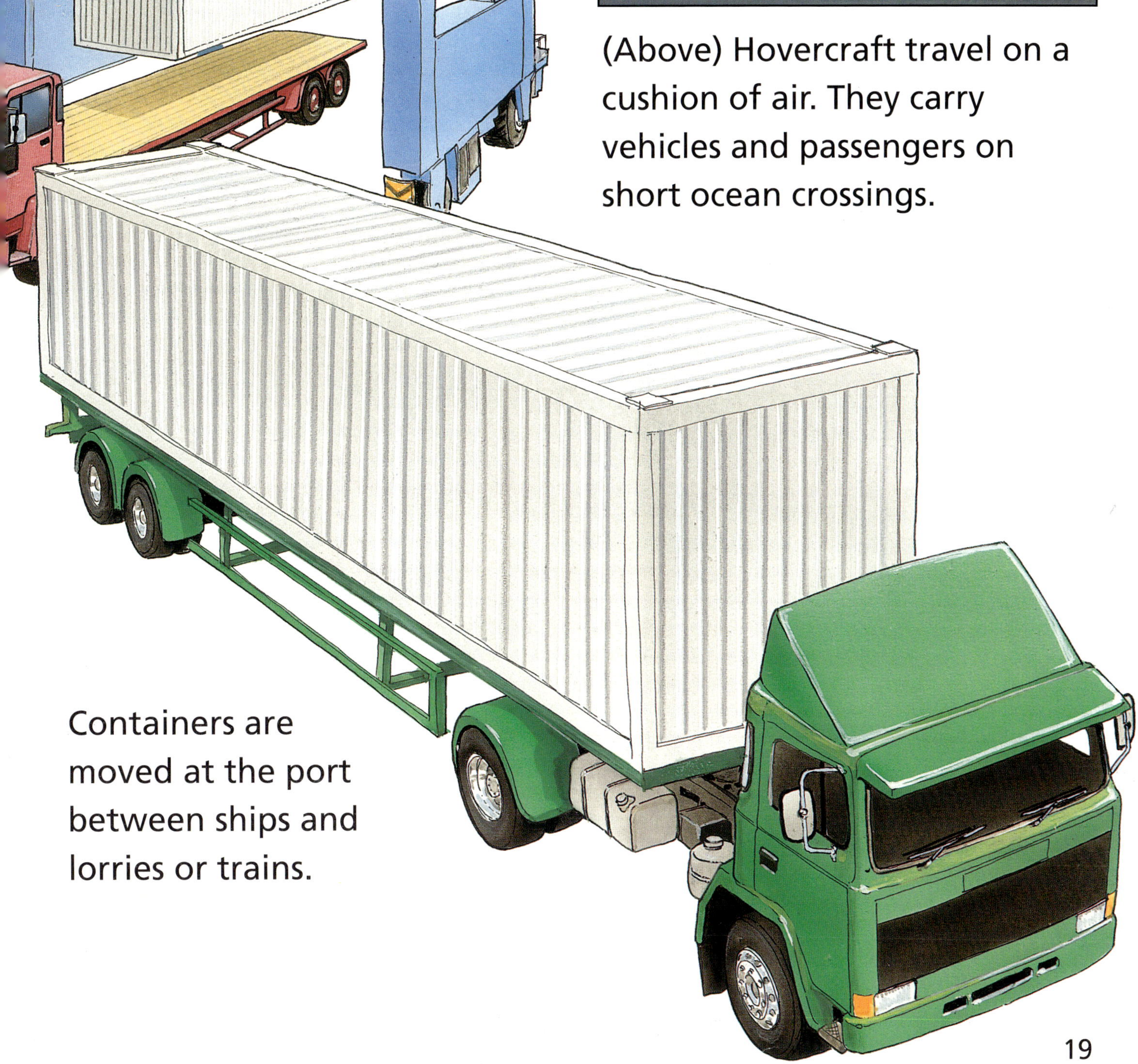

Containers are moved at the port between ships and lorries or trains.

Inland Waterways

Inland waterways are water 'roads' along which boats can travel. Most waterways are rivers but some, made by people, are canals. In Britain, canals are quite narrow but elsewhere, canals such as the Panama Canal in Central America, are large enough for ocean-going ships.

Barges usually transport goods on inland waterways. Some have their own engines, but many are moved by powerful tug boats.

(Below) Barges on canals can travel up and down hills through locks.

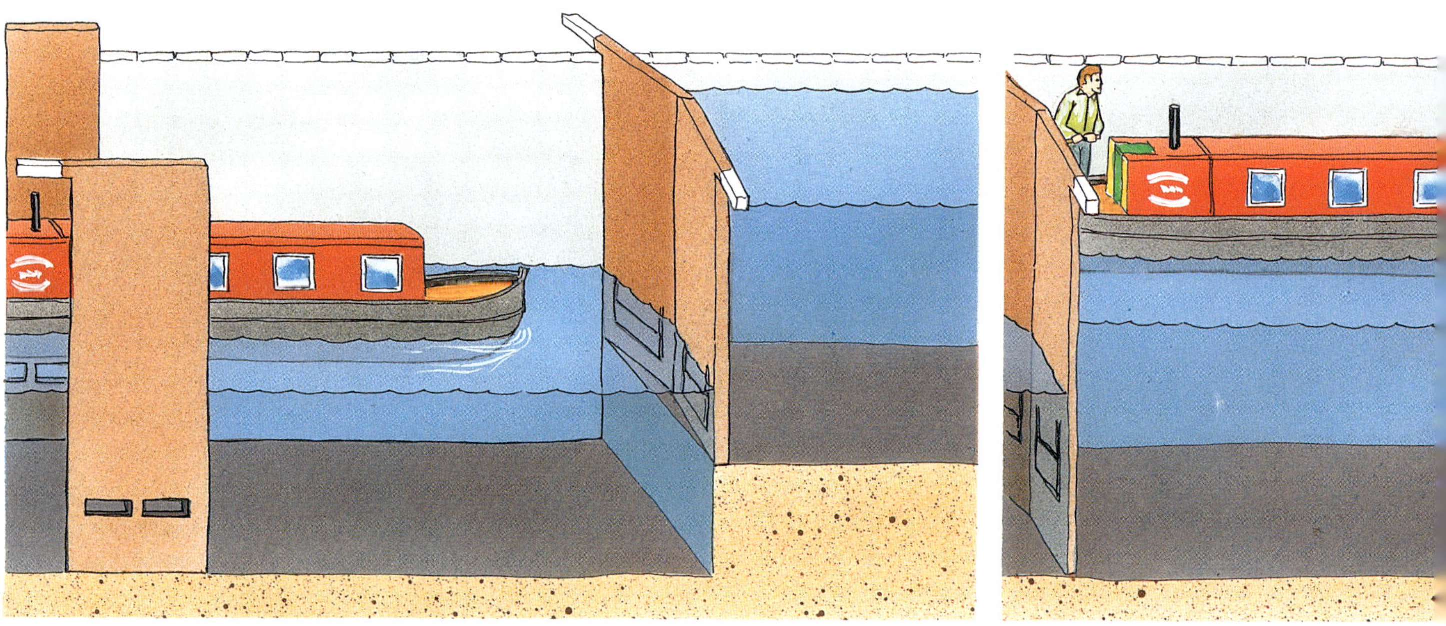

1 lower gates opened to allow the boat in

2 both gates closed, the water level rises

(Above) A ferry boat is loaded with bricks on the Madeira River in South America.

(Left) A tug boat pushes two heavy barges upstream on the River Danube in Austria.

3 upper gates opened, boat moves out of the lock

Beneath the Sea

Submarines are vessels that can travel underwater. The largest are nuclear submarines. These are fighting machines that can lurk deep in the ocean ready to fire their deadly missiles at the enemy.

Smaller submarines, called submersibles, are used by scientists to explore wrecked ships and discover wildlife living on the sea-bed.

They carry powerful lights as the deep sea is very dark.

(Right) The *Lusitania* sank off the coast of Ireland in 1915. The wreck was explored by small submersibles in 1993.

(Left) Underwater, plants and animals soon occupy a wrecked ship.

Flying High

One of the fastest ways to travel is by aeroplane. Jet aircraft fly up to 900 kilometres per hour. Concorde cruises at over 2,000 kilometres per hour. It can transport its passengers across the Atlantic Ocean in just a few hours.

Helicopters cannot travel as far or as fast as aeroplanes. But they can hover and land on the same spot, so they have special uses, such as rescuing people in danger at sea or on mountainsides.

(Right) This plane was in use in 1919. Skis allowed it to move on snow.

(Left) Helicopters can manoeuvre quickly and easily close to the ground in a way that is impossible for aeroplanes.

Hang gliders launch themselves from cliffs and hillsides.

A glider does not have an engine. It is towed into the air by a small plane. Then it finds warm currents of air to lift it high up.

(Above) A jet aircraft lands in Hong Kong among the tall buildings.

Lighter than Air

Before aeroplanes were invented, some people made journeys in hot-air balloons. Today people ride in them for fun. They have no engines and float in the direction the wind is blowing.

Airships are large balloons that have an engine and a control room hanging beneath them. Airships are filled with a gas called helium which is much lighter than air.

(Left) The air inside a hot-air balloon is heated by a burner. The air inside the balloon expands and becomes lighter than the air outside. This makes the balloon rise into the air.

(Left) In 1783 two French brothers, Jacques and Etienne Montgolfier, launched the first hot-air balloon to carry people.

(Below) Airships are often used by companies to advertise the goods that they make.

Into Space

The first human being travelled in space in April 1961. Today, space shuttles and Soyuz spacecraft often set off to orbit the Earth where they collect information about the Earth and the universe.

Soyuz spacecraft take fresh crews to the Russian Mir space station and then usually return to Earth with the old crew. The American space shuttles return to Earth with the same crew but the shuttles can be used many times.

(Right) On space walks, astronauts wear space suits and carry air packs to supply them with oxygen.

A Soyuz spacecraft approaches the Mir space station.

A space shuttle returns to Earth like a glider.

The Mir space station first went into orbit in 1986.

Word List

Arctic The region around the North Pole which is mostly frozen sea.

Burner The part of a gas-jet from which a flame rises.

Cable cars Passenger cars drawn along the road by strong cables, or cabins moved through the air by cables up a mountain.

Cargo The load carried by a train, ship or aeroplane.

Crew The people who run a ship, aircraft or spacecraft.

Cruises Journeys made by ship for pleasure.

Currents Water or air moving in a certain direction.

Distress flares Devices like rockets that are carried by boats and other craft. They are let off to alert rescue services if the craft is in danger.

Ferries Boats which carry passengers or goods across narrow stretches of water.

Helium A very light gas.

Jet aircraft An aircraft with an engine that expels a jet of hot gases backwards to propel the aircraft forwards.

Life-jacket A special safety jacket that will keep you afloat in water.

Lock A series of gates in a canal which allow boats to travel up and down hill.

Luxuries Things that are expensive and for enjoyment but not necessary.

Missiles Objects fired from a machine.

Monorail A railway on which the trains run on a single rail.

Orbit The path of a satellite circling around a planet or a planet around the sun.

Poisonous fumes Harmful gases or smoke made by the engines of vehicles.

Polluted Made dirty.

Road trains Lorries pulling one or more large trailers.

Space station A spacecraft that permanently orbits the Earth.

Submerge To sink.

Traffic The cars, buses, bicycles and lorries which use roads.

Tourists People who travel on holiday.

Vehicles Machines that carry passengers or goods on land or in space.

Vessels Hollow structures that carry passengers or goods on water.

Finding Out More

Places to Visit

Darlington Railway Museum, North Road Station, Darlington DL3 6ST

National Motor Museum, Beaulieu, Hampshire

The Canal Museum, Stoke Bruerne, Towcaster, Northants NN12 7SE

The London Transport Museum, Covent Garden, London WC2E 7BB

The National Maritime Museum, Romney Road, Greenwich, London SE10 9NF

Books to Read

Canals and Waterways, Chris Oxlade, (Watts, 1994)

Flying Machine, Andrew Nahnm, (Dorling Kindersley, 1990)

Journeys, Paul Bennett, (Wayland, 1993)

Land and Sea Transport, Hugh Johnstone, (Gloucester Press, 1989)

Space Shuttles, Ian Graham, (Watts, 1989)

Transport, Robin Kerrod, (Wayland, 1991)

Transport Around the World, Godfrey Hall, (Wayland, 1995)

Transport Machines, Norman Barrett, (Watts, 1991)

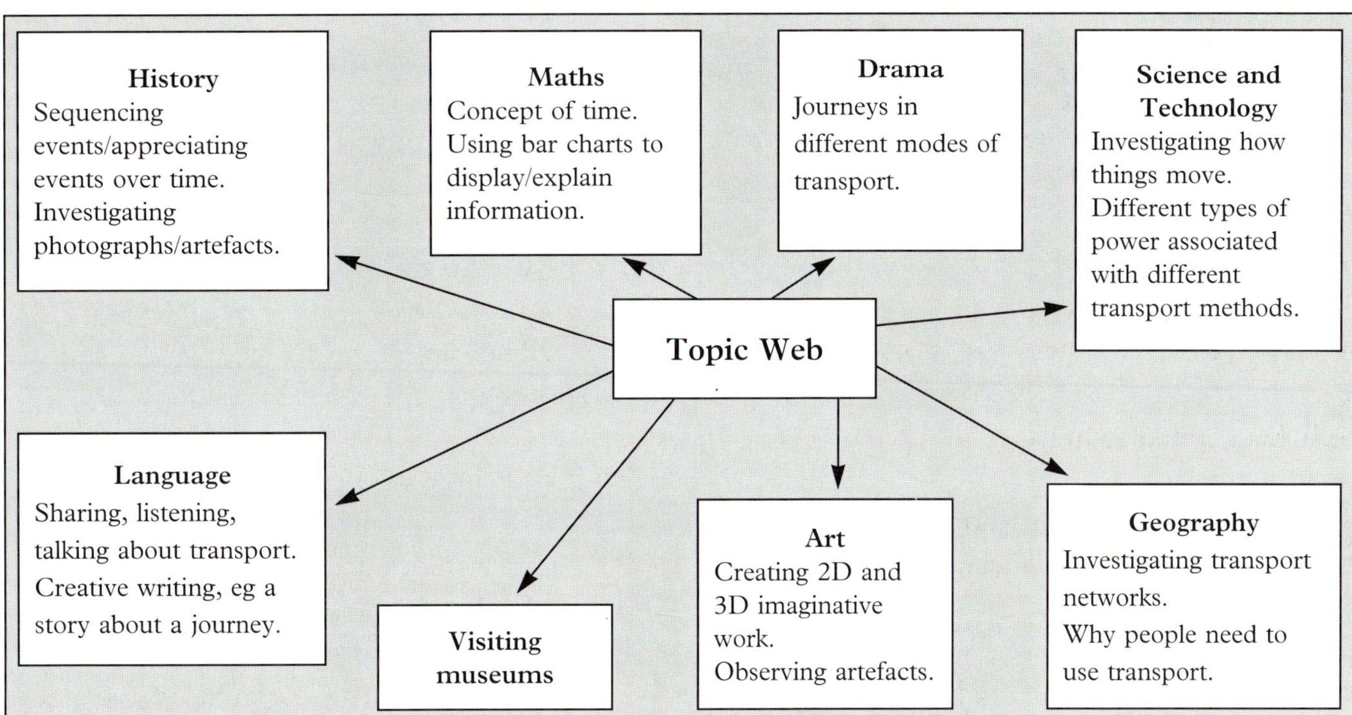

Index

Page numbers in bold *show that there is an illustration on that page.*